T ♡ **W9-AAK-642**

Thank you for
listening with
a poet's ear.

Meg Stolsky,
9-25-13

Longing for
the Blessing

Books by Judith Sarah Schmidt

Self-Help
How to Cope with Grief   (1989)

Poetry/Prose
Longing for the Blessing   (2013)

Longing for the Blessing

Midrashic Voices from Toldot

poems and prose by
Judith Sarah Schmidt

Time Being BookS

An imprint of Time Being Press
St. Louis, Missouri

Time Being Books
10411 Clayton Road
St. Louis, Missouri 63131

Time Being Books® is an imprint of Time Being Press®, St. Louis, Missouri.

Time Being Press® is a 501(c)(3) not-for-profit corporation.

Time Being Books® volumes are printed on acid-free paper.

ISBN 978-1-56809-217-1 (paperback)

Library of Congress Cataloging-in-Publication Data:

Schmidt, Judith Sarah.
    Longing for the Blessing : Midrashic Voices from Toldot / by Judith
Sarah Schmidt. — First edition.
        pages cm.
    ISBN 978-1-56809-217-1 (pbk. : acid-free paper) 1. Jewish poetry.
2. Midrash—Poetry. I. Title.
    PS3619.C4456L66 2013
    811'.6—dc23

                                                          2013023551

Cover design by Jeff Hirsch
Cover art, "Longing for the Blessing," by Jerome Kerner
Book design and typesetting by Trilogy M. Mattson

Manufactured in the United States of America
First Edition, first printing (2013)

My love and gratitude to Blanche and Irving Stiker, my mother and father, of blessed memory. Modah ani, *for you gave me the breath of life.*

My daughter Leslie, of blessed memory, modah ani, *for giving me the sweet taste of milk and honey and for guiding my vision.*

My deep gratitude to Louis Brodsky and Time Being Books, for inviting me to publish this writing. L.D., modah ani.

On the Writing of Midrash

". . . every artist paints himself."
— Cosimo de Medici

In the Ethics of the Fathers, we are instructed, with regard to the portion, to "turn it and turn it, for everything is in it."

Gerald Bruns, in Midrash and Allegory: The Beginning of Scriptural Interpretation, tells us "If the text does not apply to us it is an empty text . . . we take the text in relation to ourselves, understanding ourselves in its light, even as our situation throws its light upon the text, allowing it to disclose itself differently, perhaps in unheard-of ways."

In 2003, as I approached my seventieth birthday, I decided to be bat torah. The Torah portion I received to live with for that year was Toldot: Generations. I spent the year deep in study, reading many sources that informed me and inspired me. This study was absorbed into my midrashic meditations on the portion. Since I never intended to publish this writing, I did not keep a record for footnotes and annotations. If I have overlooked giving credit to any source, I ask to be forgiven and I give thanks for being enriched by you.

The "voices" of Isaac, Rebecca, Jacob, and Esau contained in these pages are the voices I have heard as I lived, this past year, with the Torah portion of Toldot. I have not only turned it and turned it; more often than not, it has turned and turned me. Our Torah opens ancestral doors through which I find them and also find myself in them and through them.

I take full responsibility for the "voices" in the following pages, as paintings of my own self. Aware of the ancient and sacred character of the text, I hope that what I have written does not offend anyone with a more traditional orientation to midrash. If I have, please teach me the voices of your turning and turning.

— Judith Sarah Schmidt

Contents

Longing for
the Blessing

Introduction

Judith Sarah Schmidt has created an extraordinary work. By extraordinary I mean not only to say that it is wonderful — which it is — but to put the reader on notice that this work is outside the ordinary. Whatever one might ordinarily expect a work of Biblical commentary, or poetry, or memoir, or spiritual autobiography to be, this is something else.

The voices in *Longing for the Blessing: Midrashic Voices on Toldot* are the voices of the Biblical patriarchs and matriarchs: Abraham, Isaac, and Jacob; Sarah, Rebecca, Rachel, and Leah. But because this is a work of *midrash* — a rabbinic art form which searches for meaning in Holy Writ through the creation of imagined dialogue and extension of narrative — the voices are startlingly fresh, achingly real.

Schmidt inhabits and voices each character, or perhaps it might be truer to say that the characters inhabit her and voice her. In any event, she seems to know them intimately, presents them to us without contrivance, as if speaking from a place deep within their lived experience.

As anyone who has read the Hebrew Bible knows, the characters and stories are emotionally complex. Traditional rabbinic hermeneutics tends to follow one of two paths: either to attempt to smooth out the textual difficulties, presenting the reader with an interpretation which makes the story more readily digestible, the characters less-complex (leaving us, more or less, with "good guys" and "bad guys"); or to confront the text as it actually presents itself, embracing the profound messiness of the stories and the characters. Schmidt has chosen the latter, much less traveled path.

It's an act of great courage. Schmidt does not flinch. Here are tales of heartbreak, disappointment, anger, and reproach; alongside, within, and without stories of passion, desire, longing, and love. The characters walk in light; each inevitably with their decidedly dark shadow. Later, when she inhabits the voices of her more immediate and direct ancestors, the struggling, oppositional twins of happy and sad bump up against each other so hard, each wanting "the blessing of the wholeness of existence," that they become — or so it seems, at least for a moment — one.

Schmidt has given us a work of stunning insight, remarkable intimacy, and poetic grace.

The Talmud (Sanhedrin 19b) states that whoever teaches Torah to another's child is considered that child's parent. In this way, all of us who will read from, learn from, and teach from this work are Judith's children. What an honor it is to have been asked to write these words of introduction. On behalf of all us who are already blessed to know her and to have learned from her, "Judala, you will never know how much we love you."

Rabbi Mark Sameth
8 Iyyar 5773

Toldot, My Generations: Canaan

On Mount Moriah

Isaac, I know that you went up the mountain with your father. But nowhere have I heard that you came down the mountain with him. Did you come down the mountain with your father?

No, I did not come down the mountain with my father.

Why not?

I was not able to leave the mountain.

Why not?

What happened on top of the mountain was devastating to me. Not as you think, not about the knife and Abraham's willingness to sacrifice me. No, not that story. Another thing happened on the top of Mount Moriah which affected me and my children for the rest of our lives.

Going up the mountain, with my father that morning was a silent walk. We did not speak. I noticed that my father carried no kindling for the animal sacrifice, and I thought that strange. The desert grasses were yellowed from the heat of the sun. Even at the early hour, the air was parched. We were thirsty and stopped several times to drink, but still we did not talk.

Before we reached the top of the mountain, my father turned to me, placed his hands on my shoulders and said, "My beloved son, I want you to see as I have seen, to see the One, with your own eyes. You are the flesh of my flesh, and now you will be spirit of my spirit. This is your heart's circumcision, only yours. On the top of the mountain you will meet my God, who will be your God, the One God. I will come with you, for you will need my protection. I will stand behind, but then you must proceed on your own, to behold what I have beheld on my own. This God will meet us only as we come across the threshold alone and in our own bare footsteps."

The servants were left behind. My father and I went ahead. When we reached the top of the mountain, my father grew even more silent and solemn. He drew his knife. He held it up to the heavens, and I saw it glint with a crystal light that I have never seen before. It shone upon my father's face, and I trembled to see the light upon my father from both deep within him and shining upon him, from some mysterious source I knew nothing of.

As I beheld my father raising his knife to the heavens, I believed him to be praying, to be making an offering of his knife, for my sake. I beheld him beseeching God, for my sake, offering to sacrifice his knife if only his God would show Himself to his beloved son.

Then I saw my father lower his knife and with his face still shining he backed away from me and gently pushed me forward, into the place he had been standing. Suddenly, as I stood there, I saw a whirling white light, a tunnel of light, spinning toward me. In that instant, I feared that it would take me from my body and sweep me up, into it, and take me away from this earth. I screamed and threw myself back toward my father, and I fell to the ground.

You see, I was too young, too unprepared for such a meeting with my father's God. For a moment, my father was enraged with me. In his disappointment he raised his knife to my throat. He screamed to me, with anguish, "How can you do this to my God? How can you turn away from Him?"

In that moment, an angel came, like a faint breeze in the stilled air.

"Let your son Isaac be now. You should have protected him. He was too young to behold such light. He will not be able to look again. Even the angels cried for him. It will not be for him to see your God. It will have to wait for his son and his son's son."

My father wept. He looked at me through his tears, and he saw me, with his heart. He saw that I was in fear and trembling. He saw that I was only a boy. He saw that my eyes were a wide, blinded chasm of terror, for having seen that whirling light. He saw that my skin had been stripped thin and become as white as a desert flower. My father felt sorrow for pushing me toward God before I was prepared to take the steps.

My father feared for me. He took me and placed me in a darkened cave. Then he brought a ram that had been caught in a nearby thicket. The ram covered me with its soft, hairy coat, giving my skinless self a covering while I slept. My father left me water to drink. He went down the mountain and did not return for three days and nights.

In that cave, I slept for three days and nights and dreamed into my future. I dreamed that I would have two sons. One of them would be hairy, carrying the needed protection for meeting the power of God. The other would be of a more delicate nature, through whom God's light would enter. I dreamed that these two sons were truly one son, double natured, both needed for the journey toward God.

My father returned for me and, together, we went down the mountain. I walked very slowly beside him, and he slowed his pace for me. He was no longer angry. He had a heart of mercy for me and knew that I was not like him and never would be. He devoted himself to provide me with a life that I could live, tending his wells. He regretted always his wounding of me and the way in which he caused me almost to lose myself.

When we came home, my father led me to my mother's tent. He knew it would hold the same warmth and darkness as the cave for as long as I needed it. I never did see as clearly as I did before I went up Mount Moriah. I could never again look directly into anything or anyone and so was unable to know people for who they truly were, in their hidden depths. I tried to see, but a blinding had overtaken me. This dullness in my seeing served as my cave. I like dark and dimmed places. I prefer the depth and hidden spaces of wells and caves to the open, lit-up places of the mountains.

Do not doubt that a person should meet their God with great fear and trembling. I can tell you: one must practice first and for a long time, by looking at things aslant.

Start by beholding the grape, the glistening grape that becomes the wine. Start with the slender shaft of wheat that becomes the bread. Start with beholding the gentle light in all that sits so simply upon your table.

Akeda

Dear father,
if you had known,
   on that day
   when you lifted the knife,
      razor sharp, glistening
         in the noonday desert sun,
to my young, clean throat . . .

If you had known,
      on that day
      when you stood so straight,
         prepared, with dignity,
      to sacrifice me to the
         glory of *your* God . . .

If you had known,
      on that day, father,
      that others would say,
      "No, it was not his son Isaac
         on the altar, that day.
      No, it was the other son;
   Ishmael was his perfect offering,
         whom he so loved,
         as sacrifice unto his God" . . .

If you had known,
      on that day,
      able to see into the far future,
      when other fathers
      of the tribe of Ishmael
      who love their sons as you loved me
      would be proud to wrap him
      in prayer shawls of dynamite —
      human bombs offered
      on the altar of their God . . .

If you had known,
   on that day, my father,
Would you have done different?
Would you have lifted me from that altar,
*

clasped me to your heart
and fled, with me, from the
awe of that akeda
   of all akedas?

   With all honoring,
   your son Isaac.

Who Is Standing in Front of Me?

Who is standing in front of me? Which son? It is Jacob's voice I hear, but it is Esau's hairy arms I am touching. Jacob is asking for my blessing. How can I give a blessing when I am so blinded that I do not know which son is standing before me? My blindness imprisons me. After being on Mount Moriah, with my own father, Abraham, I came down the mountain, with the blindness of not wanting to see what shook me like thunder.

It was too much for me, as a young boy, to see that my father was prepared to sacrifice me, for his faith. To see that his faith meant more to him than I did. To see that, in that moment, I did not exist for him. Oh, yes, I know the story that Abraham was tormented all the way up the mountain. Yes, I could sense that something was very wrong with him: his head bent low, his silence, his slowed and suddenly faltering step.

But think of me, walking up that mountain, so trustingly, by his side. He said come and I came. To walk up the mountain with my father was everything to me. Even if he was preoccupied, I was so deeply proud to be at his side. When he said lay down, I lay down, not knowing that I was to be the sacrifice of his faith, to his God.

My father did not bless me. Still, I remained his good son. After all, look at what happened to Ishmael. I, too, could be sent out to the desert. I could not understand, then, that the depth of my father's faith was being tested and that he was surrendering to the test because of his love for both God and me. To tell the truth, even now, as a grown man, I do not understand when people try to explain that day to me.

On that day, my mother, Sarah, saw too much as well. She was at home, waiting for us to return, having no sense of Abraham's intentions on the mountain. In the light of the candles, she saw what was about to happen. She saw the knife being lifted by my father over me. She turned away, stunned, silenced and horrified. And she saw more. She saw into the future, in which many other children would be sacrificed on the altars of faith. My poor mother became the silence of stone.

She saw, too, when she did not allow Ishmael to stay with us. She understood how each action goes on like a wave into the sea of the future. She saw into the future of that act: she saw all the brothers who would be separated from one another, exiled from one another, fighting with one another, for their blessing, for their place, their *makom*, and for their land. My mother saw too much to live. Her heart could not bear what her eyes saw. Her heart was shattered to see what life could and would bring to people.

And now, my son is standing in front of me. It is time for me to see. I must look inward, into the well of my heart. I must see clearly all that I have refused to see. I gave the seeing to Rebecca, and she took charge. My mother sent my brother Ishmael into the desert, and now my wife would send my son Esau off, like the scapegoat with the red ribbon, who has placed upon its head the unwanted blemishes and carries them into exile.

I see, now, as I look at my sons, that what is sent out to the desert returns to be reckoned with, wrestled with. I did not wrestle with my father. Perhaps if I had, he would have wrestled with God, to reverse the divine decree of my sacrifice, just as he had wrestled for Sodom and Gemmorah.

I walked in my father's shadow. I tended his wells. I see, now, how my son Jacob has lived my unlived wrestling. Even in Rebecca's womb, he wrestled for his place.

I was named laughter, but my name was not to be my destiny. I stopped laughing there, on Mount Moriah. Esau is a laugher, an enjoyer of the moment. But his laughter is not the laughter my name was meant to be, the long awaited one who brings *simcha*. Esau's laughter is the laughter of one who has given up hope, for his birthright or his blessing, and has only the moment to live for. A bowl of lentils is all he expects. Esau lives my resignation, hoping, without hope, for the blessing. Esau's laughter is the bitter laughter of despair.

Not so my Jacob. Jacob does all the wrestling I did not do. Now he is wrestling with me, for the blessing. I must give it to him, for he must go on, to complete the task of our generations of wrestling for the blessing of knowing one's place, of having one's true and authentic self.

My dear sons, Jacob and Esau, you want my blessings. It is too late for blessings. For I have already bequeathed to you the destiny of my unlived life. What I saw on the mountain was too much to see — my father not blessing me. I was afraid to lose my father's love. And so I did not wrestle with him for my blessing. I retreated, instead, into my mother's tent. There it was safe, and I drank from the well of her good heart.

My poor Rebecca. She could not hold the two inside her womb, where I planted the seeds of my light and my darkness, my unlived selves. And that light and darkness are you Jacob and Esau, my sons. You ask for my blessing. I have none to give. I have walked too much in my father's footsteps, taken care of his wells. And my eyes, having refused to see, have forgotten how to see.

Now I begin to turn my eyes inward. They cry to make a well of my self, a well of my heart. My eyes are looking inward, deep, deep into the heart of my seeing. I see you, Jacob. I see you wrestling as I did not, wrestling for the blessing. Even in the womb you were wrestling for what you wanted, and now you wrestle with me, for the blessing, and I can see that, soon, you will wrestle with the angel, for the blessing. You will wrestle for your true name and your true place, for yourself and your people.

Oh Jacob, my prayer for you, my son, is that out of all your wrestling, you receive the double heart, to hold your brother and yourself, the heart of *rachamim*.

I love you both. See my two hands, my sons, one in which to hold each of you. That is my prayer for you. Is that a blessing? I guess a blessing would be that you not have to go on this journey, which will cripple you even as you receive your blessing. But, Jacob, each son must go further on the journey than his father, to bring forth our true destiny, that all is the One.

And you, my son Esau, you are the one who has given up hope of wrestling just as I gave up hope with my father. Esau, you gave up hope for a birthright and believe you only have the moment to live for. A bowl of lentils is all you expect. Lentils will not sate your deeper hunger to be seen, to be blessed. My son Esau, you have lived my resignation, hoping without hope.

Esau, I try to see you clearly, now, my son, my son. It is difficult to do so, because I know what Rebecca wants done with you. I will have to wrestle with Rebecca, so that I can hold Jacob and you both. I must keep looking into the well of my heart. It is time for me to take my place. I will do it for you, my sons.

I will not sacrifice you Esau for, seeing you clearly, I cannot. Is that a blessing? To see one's son clearly, to see his essence distinct from all others? To see him, face to face, for all that he is and is not? That is all the blessing I would have wanted on Mount Moriah. Then my father could not have sacrificed me, for his God. I see you Esau. My hairy one. My one who lives for the moment. My son who married for the moments of pleasure, even though he married the path of exile.

No wrestling for you, Esau. You will stay here, on the land. That will be the journey of your destiny. To stay here to raise the cattle. As you tend the land and wait to see how things can be tended and grow slowly and rise up out of hidden places, you will learn about hope. Just as you subdue yourself and grow the land, Jacob will subdue and grow his heart. You will wait while he tends his heart until it becomes a womb of mercy. And when he returns, you will meet him with the gifts of your planting, and he will bring you his fruit of mercy.

And even then it will not be done. It will wait for Jacob's sons and your sons and all the sons of all the sons of your sons to complete this journey of coming together, heart to heart, face to face. And then, my dear father Abraham, and my dear mother Sarah, and my dear wife Rebecca, and myself will finally be able to rest in peace. For then you will be as One.

May my blessing be given to the generations, forward and also back into time. The exile will be over. The journey will be done. *Shema yisra'l adonay eloheynu adonay ehad*.

On the Day of My Father Abraham's Death

Everyone thinks I was a stupid, blind old man. A man who did not know what was going on around him and whose wife could pull the wool over his eyes. Let me tell you, sometimes stupidity is the best way to hide what must not be revealed. Do you know that people give off smells? If you have a smell you want to hide, like the smell of the shock of being a young boy who saw too much, it is best to hide it with another smell, like blindness.

The truth is that on the day my father died, I saw more clearly and with more wholeness and with more holiness than I ever saw before, in my life. On the day of his death, I saw with the eyes of my father, Abraham. I saw as he had wished for me to see when he took me up to Mount Moriah. But back then I was only a boy. On the day of my father's death, I became a man.

On the day of my father's death — may his name be as a blessing — Jacob was preparing the lentils of mourning when Esau returned home from hunting in the fields. Esau accepted the bowl of lentils, in exchange for his birthright. That is the truth. Esau would do such a hopeless thing as that, for he was the son of my despair. But that is not the whole truth. There is more to the story than has been revealed.

When I heard of the news of my father's death, I became delirious with grief. I could not help myself. I was back there, on Mount Moriah, as if a young boy again, with my father's hopes hanging, like a sword, over my head. To see what he saw, the One, the source of all Life, was still my whole desire. All my life, I could not bear the cloud of disappointment that I saw in his otherwise luminous eyes. Now, with my father Abraham's death, I could never give him the gift of seeing like he did and so receive his blessing that I was truly his son, his seed.

Because my young eyes had not been able to hold the abundance of such light and such love as my father wished they could, they had become shattered vessels. On the day of my father's death, I lay in bed, delirious, believing I was back on Mount Moriah, afraid I was dying. I believed I was dying both from grief for the loss of my father and because I was reliving all that was my failure on Mount Moriah. In my grief, I prayed to finally have the visions of my father that they might make me whole. As I lay dying, an angel must have seized me by the neck and, for the sake of heaven, placed me back on Mount Moriah, to finally wrestle for the blessing for my life and the lives of my sons. For I swear, I was both there, in my bed, and on Mount Moriah, at the same time.

After Rebecca got the goatskins out from the secret cave, she dressed Jacob in the skins that held the scent of the Garden of Eden where everything was One, where there was no difference between a Jacob and an Esau, where there was no war within the womb between the physical and spiritual.

My beloved Rebecca, she knew what my heart and soul yearned for before I did: to see as my father saw. She wanted to give that blessing to me, on the day of my father's death, and she wanted to give that blessing to Abraham as his spirit departed. She wanted to repair the shattering that took place on Mount Moriah that she had carried from my heart into her womb. She wanted her sons to be reconciled. She knew that for reconciliation between her sons to be possible, her husband and his father would need to find their completion.

As I lay in the bed of grief and struggled with the angel on Mount Moriah, Rebecca placed them on Jacob. Poor Jacob, he thought he was deceiving his brother and stealing his birthright.

What Jacob did not know was that, finally, Jacob and Esau would become as One, before my eyes. When Jacob came before me, in the delirium of my grief and in the fear and trembling of believing I was still on Mount Moriah, reality as I knew it had collapsed. Time past and time present, the senses of seeing and smelling, all of that merged. Now became then, seeing became smelling and smelling seeing and both became touch. That sometimes happens, you know, when the angel of death approaches.

For a short while, I smelled Esau and I heard the voice of Jacob and I was confused, unable to distinguish my sons, who were so different. But then, ah, I smelled the skins, and in a moment, it all made perfect sense. Then I could finally see. When I asked Jacob to come close, so that I could kiss him, I smelled the skins.

In the skins, I could smell the foul decay of the hairy animal. But in that smell was also wrapped the most glorious scent, a lost scent of the Garden of Eden. At that moment, I looked past my son and saw, with clearest eyes, toward the fields of heaven. I said to my son, "Look! The smell of my son." I could see beyond the limits of my senses, into his very essence.

How can I describe to you this long forgotten and unforgettable reality? How can I describe to you this moment of beholding what is hidden from us, here in this life? I can only liken it to the scent of a most fragrant rose, at once delicate and passionate with life. But it was not of a rose. I can liken it to something resembling the color blue, like the lost sublime dye of the Garden. But it was not of blue. It is not a taste or a smell or a sight that anyone can describe to anyone else. It can only be encountered on one's own, as my father well knew, and sometimes only in the bed of one's darkest grief.

When I touched that scent, I touched the dew of the fields of Shekinah. In that moment, all was restored to wholeness, to the Tree of Life. If only that moment, *dayanu*. Finally, in that moment, I saw like my father had seen, smelled like he had smelled. Finally, I was in the field of blessedness, with my father. And with my sons. May those moments remain as a blue thread of blessed memory, to guide me and my sons along our journeys.

And may my father, Abraham, know how, in that moment of *tikkun*, his life was fulfilled. May he rest in the peace of knowing his life to be our guiding vision.

Hearing the Voice of Jacob/Yaakov

Jacob's Desire

Desire began
  as I rooted
  and swam
  in the dark river
  of your womb.

I wrestled
  with your bloody currents
    the way the bud
      riots to burst
        into bloom,
    the way the salmon
      drives upstream,
        delirious
          to reach home.

Mother, forgive me.
I only quaked within you
  not to be bound
to be blessed
  in your doorway,
    delivered, freely,
      into the passion
        of being.

I did not know
  how it was for you,
    to be wounded by me,
    until I became a man
  and spent a starless sleep
    at the crossing
      of the river Jakkob,
    where I wrestled
      with the One I could not see.

You can find the sign
  of the blessing
    bestowed, that night,
  upon the limp of my right leg.

Tell me, my mother,
  why must my every blessing
    issue forth from
    a wounding
      and a long wandering,

  until, as in a dream,
    my heart crowns
      releases into peace,
    finally able to hear
      the heavens sing
        the sacred sound
          of my soul's true name?

Learning from Jacob

It is said, in Ethics of the Fathers, that when involved in the practice of midrash, we are to turn and turn the portion around and around until we have extracted all kind of essence that is contained for us within the portion.

During this year of living with the portion given me for my bat torah, and the wider story of Esau's and Jacob's journey surrounding it, I have found myself not only turning the story but being turned by it, in sudden and surprising ways.

I am driving my car on the highway, focused on the traffic around me, when, out of the blue, I hear strong words spoken to me: "well of course it would be Jacob and not Esau who would receive the blessing. After all, it is Jacob who would know how to use it. Why should a blessing go to someone who would settle for a bowl of lentils?"

This came to me as an utterly surprising and unacceptable message and went against everything I had consciously thought about Jacob and Esau. Until this moment, I had seen the situation of the twins with what I thought was clarity. I saw Jacob as a deceiving trickster, conniving and in concert with his mother to do whatever he had to do to extract the blessing from his father that rightfully belonged to his brother, Esau.

Now, from out of nowhere, I have been directed to consider things from the diametrically opposite viewpoint. Jacob is not a thief. Instead, he is the only one of the twins who could possibly be considered for the blessing. The voice is essentially telling me that I am quite the dope not to see the obvious right before my eyes.

I am no longer turning and turning the portion. Suddenly it is turning me. "Go inside", it is saying, "surrender yourself, to look at yet another facet of this soul story that is shaping you."

When I arrive home, I become quiet, enter into receptive meditation and wait to receive whatever understanding will come. I hear the voice of Jacob.

Do not think of me as a character in some family drama, although I am. Do not think I am some mythic being whose story you can analyze and tear apart with your good thinking, although you can.

Think of me, rather, as you. No, not just a part of you, but as circulating in the very particles of your being, your ancestor coursing through your blood. If you come to meet me in all of my complexity, you will be sure to meet your own self.

I, and therefore you, come from roots that hold the opposites of being, the struggling diversities of this physical plane of reality. Strife is part of our very nature. Who knows this better than me, from the time in the womb, in turmoil with Esau?

In my mother's womb, the angel showed me how, in life, I would struggle with my own shadow self, my twin, my opposite. The angel showed me the way of right relationship with my opposing twin. And then she placed her finger over my lips, and in that moment, I forgot.

As we were leaving the womb of Rebecca, I still held a trace of how I needed to be with my brother, my twin self. At the doorway, my hand still in the womb, still close to the angel, I held Esau's heel, with love. I was loving him, and I was guiding him. I was a true brother.

You see, even then I knew that Esau needed me to guide him. Even in the womb, he was pushed about by his urges. They surged through him and stormed the whole space of mother's womb. I was more capable than Esau of being still, of seeing, of having vision. I could hold him. He could not hold me. He could not even contain himself. We each have these parts, one that is filled with raw urge, our animal *nefesh* soul. And another soul is ours, too, our *neshumah*, or higher soul, connecting us toward a vision of the One.

Judith, do you not know your twin selves, your nefesh *and your* neshumah *selves? Your own urges that storm through you? Some of them surge so strongly that they control your whole life, do they not — urges for power, for success, for sex, for food, to be loved at any cost? Do these not, at times, storm through your own life and too often take over the self of you who knows better? The* neshumah *who knows more than just the moment of desire, who has the capacity to see the whole picture and act for the higher and deeper good, to act for the sake of heaven.*

I was holding his heel with love and then, in a flash of a moment, my hand was out of the womb and the loving touch turned to a struggle for who would be born first, who would be preferred, who would be blessed. With my hand, I was pushing him back into the womb. In a moment, love was torn apart and turned into a lust for power, position and recognition. In that moment, we became brothers who were doomed to be enemies.

Judith, do you not know, in your own life, how you wield power over your own twin self? Do you not know how you hate it, berate it, try to put it away somewhere, not to be born into the light of day? Do you not know about self-hatred and self-exile of your twin self, fearing that if it is seen, it will prove you to be lesser?

Do you not know how you see your twin self in another person or in another group of people and treat them no different than you treat the twin within you? Do you not know the havoc that threatens to wreck our world from this way of relating to our brothers and sisters in ourselves and others?

My whole life has been a journey toward remembering how, at the beginning, my love was upon him like a strong and guiding hand, without judgment or condemnation. You are right to judge me for deceiving my twin and stealing his birthright, but you are wrong to think it did not have to be wrestled for. See, now you have to hold these opposing ways of looking, for both carry the truth.

It is important to be a wrestler. However, I have learned, the hard way, that one does not have to be an attacker or a deceiver to be a wrestler. It is important only that the truth be wrestled for. It was important that I wrestle Esau for the birthright, for the responsibility of passing on our lineage, for the truth was that Esau was not capable of that. And there is a part of each of us that must carry the vision for the other.

Judith, isn't there a part of you who would settle for a bowl of lentils instead of holding out for the greater blessing? Do you not know how powerful this settler for less can be in your life, especially when this twin has been disowned and no longer expects more than a bowl of lentils?

The Esau part of each one of us needs to be wrestled with but not attacked and rejected. I came to know, in the course of my life, that each part of us is a surging wave of light and life and no part of life must be attacked or disowned. Guided, yes, but not attacked. Any part of us that is attacked or exiled will cast a long shadow outside of us and will be met elsewhere, in another. This I found out through the twenty years I spent living with Leah and Rachel, sisters as opposite as Esau and I, and with Laban, who outsmarted me as trickster and deceiver. In Haran, the shadow that I tried to disown and run from in Canaan caught up with me.

By hating and attacking and deceiving our inner twin or our twin in any other person, we negate a current of life. God knows I negated Esau and many others, time and time again. I have had to learn by serving Laban, my own shadow self, for many years of my life how what I distance from myself, I meet in another, no matter how far away from myself I travel.

It took me most of my life. It took having the face of God revealed to me, at Pineal, and it took wrestling with the angel at the river Jabbok, who would not let go of me until my heart cracked open. It took beholding the radiating mystery of life to open to my heart. And it took being wounded and limping into my future to become a whole man of heart. There I was called Israel, "seeker," and could hear the faint whisper of the *Sh'ma* — "Hear, O Israel, the Lord our God is One." Only in the vessel of the heart can all that is an opposing two become the One.

You know that on the Tree of Life, I am given the honor of residing in the place of the heart, called Tiferet. I am grateful to be acknowledged for the wrestling with myself and with my twin and with my demons, to have been brought home to my heart. The heart is not an encapsulated organ within our body. It is a large and radiating and pulsating part of the very force of life, living at the very center of us and of our universe.

The heart is where we come to in the process of holding all the opposites of our being and of our world. If we can hold all the twin selves in the flowing space of the heart, we can find a way toward a never before known reconciliation that arises out of its mysterious current of creation. The heart is the great alchemical vessel of life, for it turns the forces of duality into the gold of the One.

I proceeded to meet my brother Esau after wrestling for the blessing at the river. We met and embraced and held each other in the great womb of the heart. In this way, we repaired the first womb in which we struggled. In this way, we gave one another our brotherly blessings. You may wonder why, after such a profound reconciliation with Esau, I did not remain to live with him, in the same place.

Judith, don't you know how it is best not to get so close to those parts of us, or people we love, that can seduce us and take us over and destroy our vision? Know that it is essential to embrace our troublesome twins, inside and out, but not to live too close to them. Distance and perspective are required for any vision to remain a strong and guiding force for the One.

It is necessary to have the perspective of distance that allows you to take all the opposites into an open heart. The heart is a doorway where all is bathed in the great silence of the One and breathed into new life.

Wherever I may be, Esau will be in my heart. Still, I must live at some distance from him so that he cannot hold sway over me. Esau, too, is grateful that I did not succumb to his weakness, for he, too, wants nothing more than wholeness, and for that he needs to trust that, for the sake of heaven, I can hold enough distance to wrestle with and guide him along our way.

Judith, stay open to receiving my voice and the voices of all you Torah ancestors for we are here to guide you. As you see, we may come at the strangest of time, such as when you are driving your car. So, one last word: pay attention, drive safely.

Hearing the Voice of Esau

Esau's Sacrifice

My mother made a sacrifice of me.
Even before I was born,
      I was the one she chose.
She had her reasons.
As she came to know
      my lusty kick
      against the walls of her womb,
      she knew what my life could serve.

My mother knew what my father needed.
After he came down from Mount Moriah,
      He thought too often of rams.
He dreamed of rams
      rising out of thorny thickets,
      placed on stone altars,
         burned instead of him,
         throats cut and bloodied.

If not rams, other animals would do.
Just as long as there was
      a daily four-legged sacrifice.
After Mount Moriah, my father believed
      that each new day
      would spare him only
      if it was given a hairy offering,
      just as on the day
      when he and his father were alone
      on top of that windy, whirling mountain.

When my mother saw me,
      she looked upon me,
      with her knowing smile.
I was the hairy twin,
      the one to be put to good use,
      to play the role
      in the daily drama
      of father's redemption

My hairiness became
      my father's trusted reminder
      that his life would be spared,
      for yet another day.
I became his hunter, his deliverer.
I did not mind, for I loved my father.
I even cooked for him.
It calmed him to see
      me turn the sacrifice
      and his terror
      into a daily delicacy.

I only minded that after all I did
      for my mother,
      for her love of my father,
she never looked beneath
      my ruddy, hairy self,
      never found me
         behind my lonely eyes.

If only she had sung her dream to me,
      her song, rising out of her breath,
      like the first sound of the world,
If only she could have held me
         in the fields
         where I hunted,
         carrying the
         weight of the animal
         and father's despair,
      had warmed me
         in the desert,
         through the cold
         and starless nights.

Esau Walks Alone and Talks to the Stars in the Night Sky

When you left, my brother, I waited for the dawn of the next day, and then I, too, left our family. Like you, I fled and entered the desert, alone. Unlike you, I had no place to go. My mother did not send me to safety. I did not know where I was going. I wandered.

I never told you that I suffered from a terrible starvation. Even when I would eat some of a delicacy I had prepared for our father, I would still be starving. Jacob, starvation ruled my life. That is why I sacrificed my blessing, for the bowl of lentils you offered me. My starvation made me desperate.

In the desert, I feared starvation. I looked for manna. Sometimes I would find a desert plant and would suck the moisture and nourishment from it. It was like a mother's milk. But there was so very little of it, I came to crawl across the sands, with dry mouth and empty stomach. At times, I was so hungry that I craved even the sand.

Wherever I looked I saw endless blurred space. I would not stop moving, for fear of never starting again. I promised myself that when the next pain of starvation came, I would stop, put my face on the hot sands, and allow myself to become whitened bones, driftwood, in the desert. I knew that my bones would never be sought, nor found, nor carried out of exile.

The sun was unrelenting. A large red ball loomed over the desert sands. The heat made everything before my eyes ripple like waves of the sea. Strange, in all the dryness of the desert, I felt like a drowning man. As I struggled, I could recognize some shape, some form beckoning me forward. I said to myself that in my delirium I was seeing a mirage and looked away.

When the hunger pains began again, I stopped moving. I lay my head on a stone in the sand. I surrendered myself to dying, becoming bare bone. I dreamed of being on an oasis in the desert. Where there was a pool of clear water and a palm tree. Under the palm tree sat an old woman. She beckoned me to sit beside her. She said that her name was Deborah and that she had been my mother's nursemaid.

She said that she had come from the house of Laban, where Jacob now lived. She said that she had been summoned by our

mother, Rebecca, to come to me. She fed me fruit from the tree
and cupped her hands with water from the pool for me to drink.
She was a source of sacred comfort to me, for she seemed to
know me. She told me to keep looking out toward the sun, for
what I had seen was meant for me and was no mirage.

When I opened my eyes, I stared ahead, toward the sun,
toward whatever it was that appeared in the intense light. In
the shimmering blur I could make out a tent in the not too far
distance. Again, exhausted, I closed my eyes and drifted. Next
I knew, I was being carried toward that tent. And then I was
inside of the tent. It was a large tent with many people in it.

Among them were my uncle Ishmael and his mother, Hagar.
They embraced me and welcomed me. They sat with me and
heard my story. For the first time, I tasted what it was like to
belong to the warmth of a family. They explained to me that
everyone who lived in the tent was like me, each having been
exiled, in one way or another, from their tribe. They themselves
had become a tribe.

They told me that the healing of my starvation would come
from drinking in the love of their tender and serious smiles.
They told me that their exile had caused them to wrestle with
the bitterness and revenge in their hearts and with the blind
desire to throw stones at those who had cast them out. They told
me that their wrestling mightily with their demons had cracked
their hearts open, into a deep well of grief, and that the bearing
of their grief opened into deeper wells of tender mercy.

I lived with them for some time. They were a very calm
people, and I could feel, deep down in their belly a quiet fire
of strength and stillness burning. They held me while I cried
and cursed and moaned the grief of losing my mother's love
and my father's blessing.

Within the time of my stay, their loving filled the hunger that
had begun in my mother's womb. They were right. That bowl of
lentils was no longer important to me. Nor was the birthright
from my father. It came to pass that nothing mattered to me
more than the light pouring through the crack in my newly
opened heart.

One day, Ishmael came to me and told me that it was time to return to my old land. He explained to me that those of our tribe were needed out in the world, to become a tent for those who were wandering, exiled. He explained to me that as long as there would be thirty-six of us, the pain of others would be softened, for by our solemn smiles the exile would find his tent and his tribe.

Jacob, my brother, may there be thirty-six of you and thirty-six of us throughout the generations, to hold the pillars of hope in our world.

For this prayer, my brother, I came, that day, to meet you and embrace you and smile upon you and forgive you. No matter where you are now, please know that you are part of me. That you and I are one in the One.

May our souls remember what our minds have forgotten: the blue threat of peace that was between us, in our beginning, in the first tent we shared, within our mother, before the wrestling. Be blessed, my brother, and may our children and our children's children know peace, as far and wide as the branches of our tree may spread.

Hearing the Voice of Rebecca/Rifka

Rebecca's Dream

I am in a green land.
The scent of myrtle trees
and the sounds of the turtle doves
　　　fill the air.
I am with my husband, Yitzhak.

We are wrapped
　　　in shimmering waters
　　　under a silken sky.

He is holding me close
　　　the way he used to.

We are moving together
　　　like luminous slippery fish.

He is sliding the stars
　　　into my dry heart.

My mouth is opening
　　　I am crying out:
　　　"Lord, fill my womb.
　　　　　Make me mother,
　　　　　Lord, make me mother."

I am swelling, I am swelling.
　　　I am becoming river.
He is still holding me

Last Will and Testament

For my sons, Jacob and Esau

To be read, by you, at the time of my death, in the cave of Machpelah, so that the peace and forgiveness of understanding may come to you and to all who come to rest in this cave.

Dear sons:

I want you to know about my life, at this time of my death. It is my hope that in knowing about my life, you will have some understanding of how I came to do the things I did to each of you.

In my old age, I was as alone and bereft as a person could be. More so than even your grandfather Abraham, when I first saw him. And I did not think that was possible. Abraham had one son return to him, but I, out of my own actions, lost both of my sons.

Please forgive me, for not loving either of you wisely, with my whole heart, but with a heart that had become hardened by my disappointed dreams.

Here, my sons, is my story.

If I had not wanted better I could have stayed in Haran, in my brother Laban's house. But I had long dreamed of another land, one of milk and honey, where I could become someone worthwhile and make a different and better life. Ever since I was a child, I felt that true home was elsewhere.

I was a beautiful woman, very intelligent, and in my youth I flowed with hope. I had developed the determination needed to grow up with my brother, Laban. I was smarter than him and yet, if I had remained living with this conniving twin, I could only become like one of his handmaids, for the rest of my life. Every waking moment, he put his thumb on me, telling me to do this and do that, just because he was a man and the firstborn, by a few seconds.

Even Deborah, my nursemaid, encouraged me to leave. She was the only one in Haran I would have stayed for, the only one who saw with clear eyes. Deborah had heard so much about Abraham in Canaan, how he had rich water wells and land and animals. The way Deborah spoke, I could see the whole place like the land of milk and honey of my dreams. At that time, nothing was known of the story of what happened on Mount Moriah.

When Abraham sent his servant, Eliezer, to bring back a woman who would be a wife for his son Isaac, I had no doubt that I would be that woman. I wept as I left Deborah. I embraced her, this warm-breasted, wise woman, who had nursed me and held me when I was a child. I wanted her to come with me, but she said she would have work to do in Haran. I should have realized, then, that Deborah was seeing into dark clouds of our future and knowing how she, in her old age, would be needed in the house on Laban and that I would never see her again.

I rode far away from Haran, early one morning, with Eliezer, following him through the desert, on a camel Abraham had sent just for me, the first sign that I would have a better life in Canaan. As we stopped to rest and drink, on the journey, I would ask Eliezer to tell me about Isaac. What did he look like? Was he a rich man like his father? Was he a wise man like his father? Was he good to his mother?

Eliezer would answer none of my questions. He just poured more water and offered another date. I may as well have sat there with a stone. And so, after a while, I closed my mouth, and we traveled in silence. "Stupid man," I thought, not to answer the questions of a woman coming, as a stranger, to a strange land and a strange husband! How impatient I was in my youthful ambition!

It was dusk as we approached Canaan. From atop the camel, I saw a man out in the distance, in the fields. I peered to make him out. He was tall. He walked slowly, his hands behind his back, his head slightly bent. His lips were moving as if he were talking to someone, but no one else was there. He did not seem to see us approaching. "Is he blind or something?" I recall asking myself. I find it very strange — those things we hear ourselves say to ourselves that seem so insignificant at the moment. Later, however, they come back to haunt us, with the clarity of our seeing and inner knowing. How did I know that Isaac was blind? Another thing like that happened in those moments, as well.

As we came closer and I looked at the figure of the man, I noticed that there was a tear in the collar of his robes, the tear of a mourner. I thought that perhaps he was mourning. More than that I remember saying to myself, "He's torn." These two words moved through me like a passing cloud and then were gone. Now, that's strange, don't you think, that from the distance, in the first moments of seeing Isaac, I saw his torn-ness?

How could I know so much about Isaac when I did not yet know him at all? After all, I'm not a Deborah or a Sarah. I am not able to see into things. And yet I saw everything, right there and then, about my future with Isaac. I saw, in that moment, that, for me, this was not to be a land of milk and honey.

It turns out that Abraham wanted a wife for Isaac as soon as possible because he was worried that his son would never come back to this side of life. You see, Abraham had just about sacrificed his son's life, up there on Mount Moriah, but Isaac was saved in the very last minute, no thanks to his father. Isaac disappeared for a whole year. During that time, his mother, Sarah, died of the heartbreak of losing her precious son, for whom she had waited so long and without whom she saw no reason to go on living.

Can you imagine what life became for Abraham when he came down from Mount Moriah? He came down by himself. Isaac stayed up there, retreated, in dread, into some dark cave. When Abraham came down and told Sarah what had happened up there, she could not forgive him. She left him and Canaan. He never saw Sarah alive again. Soon after, Abraham heard that his beloved wife had died of grief, and he went to bury her, in this very cave. Sarah was the first to find peace here.

One day, Isaac reappeared from out of nowhere. He did not seem to recognize his father, for he did not look at him, as if he were blind or as if Abraham were dead and gone, perhaps even hated. Gaunt and silent, he entered the tent of Sarah and came out only at night, to seek scant nourishment. Sometimes, he could be seen at dusk, wandering the fields, under the first stars, by himself. He seemed to be talking to someone, but there was no one there. He did not seem to notice anyone around him. This is the man I came carrying my hopes and dreams to. Little did I know that it was I who was the hope and dream of Abraham, for his son and himself and the future.

Here is what I came to: Abraham, alone and bereft in Canaan, having sent his beloved son Ishmael off, with his beloved Hagar, and now feared by his beloved son Isaac. Abraham, filled with guilt and remorse, wandering around Canaan, followed by his devoted servant Eliezer, still praying to that God of his to make things better. I could only guess that he heard his God tell him to send for a wife for Isaac and that I was to be that wife.

No wonder poor Eliezer had not answered any of my questions. He knew that if he told me all he knew, I would return to Haran, where I would have continued to resist Laban and hope for greener pastures. Poor Eliezer, he kept silent because he could not be a liar like my brother, Laban, and because he yearned to bring help to Abraham and Isaac.

Isaac and I married but, in truth, your father was not looking for a wife. Isaac stayed in Sarah's tent, close to the remains of her scent. You would have thought it was the scent of the Garden of Eden he was binding his sorrow and his very life in. It did not take long for me to see that it was not a wife Isaac sought. He wanted a substitute for his beloved mother, Sarah. He wanted a righteous woman like his mother, to adore him and take care of him, and, as you both know, I was not that woman. I regret, now, that I had not taken with me, from Haran, Deborah's ever-flowing warmth, so that I could have given it to your father and to both of you and to myself.

It was Sarah who became most important to me, in Canaan. In her death, she became a living presence for both Isaac and for me, albeit for different reasons. For me, Sarah lived and breathed as a strength that could survive and direct life forward. Wasn't it she who got rid of Ishmael? That took a lot of force over her husband, who loved both Hagar and Ishmael. And yet he followed Sarah's commands.

I devoted myself to having the same strength and determination of a Sarah, over the men in my life. I had already demonstrated that strength, in getting away from Laban. If Isaac was weak and blind, I would be the one to take charge of our lives. I needed him to give me children, preferably sons. I needed him often because I was barren.

Why was I barren? Was it because my heart and the flower of my womb had withered and turned to steel, out of disappointment and loneliness and fear in this strange land? Steel is not a place for seeds to grow. Only rarely did my heart and womb soften when Isaac came to me and held me, in love, in the night. You see, my sons, I wanted, more than anything, to be a wife and a mother, but I was proud and would not show my need. Missing and needing the generosity and enlivening of my desire, Isaac visited my tent less and less.

One night, however, was different. The moon was round and full, and he came and held me especially close, and that is when his twin seeds were delivered into my womb. *Baruch Hashem*.

There is something I came to know about your father, on that night, which you must know, so that you can fully honor him. While he embraced me, I saw Isaac's lips moving, just as they did out in the field when I thought he was talking to someone who was not there. As he held me, he whispered sounds that I knew were not for me to understand. His face was lit up. I realized that Isaac was deep in prayer as he made love to me.

And when I found myself filled with both of you, I understood the power of your father's prayers, how they could open the barren wells of my womb and my heart.

Now I knew what he was doing out in the fields by himself. I knew when I sent you, Jacob, covered in animal skins, to your father, to deceive him for the blessing, that he would know everything, through his prayers. That is no excuse for the things I did on that day, but I want you to know that I had come to honor your father. He had become like a prince, to me, a prince who was abundantly rich with the power of prayer.

Following Sarah, I sent one son away from me. I sacrificed you, my son Esau, to be your father's. He needed the strength that I already knew, in my womb, belonged to you. You were more like me, headstrong, determined to go after your desires. Isaac needed you to do the things for him that I was not willing to do. You could deliver him from his torn-ness, do for him, what I, his wife, would not do, bring his soul home, from the mountain.

And you, Jacob, you were mild. You were more like Isaac. But I needed you to be mine. I wanted to shape you in the image of my desire. I am sorry, for I did not see you for you but only for the future you could open for me, for the lost dreams you could make come true for me, in Canaan.

I did not take you up to the Mount Moriah, but I sacrificed each of you no less than Abraham had been willing to sacrifice Isaac. I sacrificed you each in a different way. You, Esau, I sacrificed by taking your birthright from you, so that I could have Jacob carry out my dreams. You, Jacob, I sacrificed to my own devices, by making you deceive your brother and your father, so that you could receive the blessings and so fulfill my dreams. Who did I think I was? God? Or was God using Jacob and me in ways I did not even know about? Was Sarah, unseen, still present, directing me?

Esau, only now can I see the pain I caused you by withdrawing my heart from you. If I had seen your pain then, I think I would have suffered from nausea and vomited it up, for it was so like my own pain of not belonging, of having hungers that would never be satisfied, of being headstrong without the quiet faith of Isaac and Jacob.

Now, I sing to you, my beloved Esau. My songs no longer belong only to Jacob. Listen, my son, listen through the silence of Machpelah, while my spirit is still here. There is a soul sound in my heart that is only for you. Listen as it radiates and sings through you. I am sorry it comes to you so late. Take it into your heart, as your inheritance, as your soul strength and birthright, and go, in peace, to find your blessing.

And you, my beloved Jacob, go forth, free of carrying the burden of my dreams upon your shoulders. Place that weight into my grave, to be buried with me, for the burden of those dreams belongs to no one but me.

One last thing I must tell you. I have never uttered this before. After you left our home, Jacob and Esau, I was as wretched as a soul can be, filled with remorse for all that my actions had wrought. I did not know where to turn. Long ago, when the two of you were in my womb and I felt I could not go on living with such inner struggle, I called out to God, *"Lama zeh anokki"* — "Why-this-I-am?" When you went away, again I cried these words out to God, with a full throat of sorrow.

The next morning, I awoke knowing what I had to do. I told Jacob that I must go off, by myself, for a few days. I asked

Eliezer to guide me as he had so long ago. I gathered some clothing and water and took the camel and proceeded toward Mount Moriah. Leaving Eliezer below, I climbed the mountain, at dawn, just as Abraham and Isaac had done so long ago. I could feel myself walking in their very footsteps. I had no idea what I was doing. I only knew that I was being guided in response to my call. I placed one foot in front of the other and followed upon the path.

When I reached the top of the mountain, I looked about for the cave that Isaac had stayed in, for I longed to hide myself in there. As I walked about in the morning light, I came upon a ram's horn lying on the earth. I lifted it and, holding it in my hands, looked into its hollow inside. I held it up and blew it and heard the sounds of my heart pierce the heavens.

Then I removed my shoes, for I felt I was standing in a holy place. I became still and silent. As I stood there, I became like the ram's horn, empty, hollow. I was wrapped in the echoes of the sounds of my prayer. I could feel myself being blown through, by the heavens. A whirling sound of light moved through the emptiness of me. I became the light and the silence. I do not know how much time passed, for all sense of time had dissolved. All around me things were lit with the light of abundant love. I understood the invisible flowing presence of the God of Abraham and Isaac as I had never understood before.

I understood that the silence of Abraham and Isaac was not only the silence of their earthly sorrows but also the deep silence of their faith in this light they had been filled with, on Mount Moriah. Now I understood the path of their invisible God and the invisible path of the heart they walked upon. I understood the light I saw upon their faces. I understood that I had been brought to Canaan to become part of this family, to see through their eyes and through the eyes of their God.

I came down the mountain very slowly. I returned to my husband. I found him in the fields, as I had first seen him, on that day so long ago. Like a bride, I covered my face, with my veils. I went to him and took his hands and kissed them. My tears of loving gratitude warmed him.

I went to Abraham and thanked him for sending Eliezer for me, so long ago.

I went to Sarah's tent and wrapped myself in her scent, as Isaac had done.

Esau, I prayed to Deborah to go and find you and bless your wandering and quell your starvation in the desert.

Jacob, I prayed for you to find your true name.

Now, my beloved sons, go forth and create blessings. Along the way, carry the blessings of your ancestors. Feel them weightless, like the breeze of Being's mystery upon your faces.

My Generations: Boibrke, Poland

Memory is a passion no less powerful or pervasive than love. What does it mean to remember? It is to live in more than one world, to prevent the past from fading and to call upon the future to illuminate it. To remember is to revive fragments of existence, to rescue lost beings, to cast harsh light on faces and events, to drive back the sands that cover the surface of things, to combat oblivion and to reject death.

— Elie Wiesel, *All Rivers Run to the Sea: Memoirs*

Hearing the Voice of Judah

Judah is the name of my paternal great-grandfather. There are only a few threads of memory of him that have been passed on to me. He was tall. He was very strong. He was a rabbi in the shtetl of Boibrke, Poland. He had a long beard. He is the grandfather of my father Isaac. My father, into his old age, had the wide-eyed look of a young boy whenever he spoke with reverence of Judah. I am named after him, Yehudit. The name means "grateful." The rest of who Judah is can be restored from oblivion only by my entering the dreamtime of midrash and hearing Judah's voice . . .

It was still wintry, but the light was already changing. I remember that, because from within the late-afternoon light of the synagogue, where I was leading the *mincha* (afternoon prayer), before Sabbath began, I looked out the window. I saw the soft light of the afternoon bathe the yellow walls. I can recall the quiet fullness deep within my belly. I loved our small sanctuary, being there with the other men, praying, singing, sharing our souls and our lives and knowing we would share one another's deaths. I recall the sweet promise of spring that filled the air as we opened the door and left just before Sabbath.

We lingered on the unpaved road outside the synagogue. We must have all felt the small bit of added warmth in the air and the light touching us, like animals who know, instinctively, when the weather is changing. We stood there together, our coat collars pulled up to our mouths, talking and laughing, shifting from one foot to the other, as we braced against the chill still in the air. None of us wanted to break the warmth of our brotherly connection before entering the female world of our family, for the Friday evening meal.

One of the men pulled a bottle of schnapps from his coat pocket, and we each passed it around the circle and drew a long swallow, to heat our stomachs. As I walked home, I carried the warmth in my belly, like a wealthy man who sits in front of his fire. I hummed, for I felt blessed. I did not know how wealthy I was, back there in the midst of our poor life that put only turnips and potato soup and black bread on our table, during the week, and gave us our portion of manna, our precious chicken, for the Sabbath.

I walked on the path in the woods, toward my small home. I looked forward to the golden scent of the braided Sabbath loaves that would still be baking when I opened the door. The light shone on the bare trees, which slanted themselves, like etchings, against the sky. As the sun went down, the sky turned an iced blue, frozen like the lake beyond the meadow. I whistled as I walked and thought that, soon, the birds would return, and whistle back to me.

I did not hear the birds, but I remember, and I can hear them still, the steps behind me, many steps moving in the woods, over the dead leaves and iced snow, making the sound of a crackling fire. As I turned to look at what was making the sound, I knew. I did not have to turn to know. I knew, already, before I saw, that I was being encircled in a trap, by what we called cossaks. This is how we named the groups of young men — thugs — who descended upon us, like big birds falling upon their prey in the forest.

I held my prayer book and my tallis (my prayer shawl), which were wrapped in the blue velvet bag I had owned for the past thirty years, since I was thirteen. There were about six of them. I can see them still, coming out from behind the trees, circling me — young men, the oldest not more than the age of my oldest son, Label, about seventeen, the youngest not more than twelve or thirteen. They were coming out from behind the trees, and as the circle they made closed around me, smaller and smaller, my breath squeezed tighter, like a rope around my chest. The younger ones hovered back, on the outside of the circle.

The tallest of them took from his coat a knife. It was long. As he lifted it, the steel of it glistened in the light that, just a few moments before, had carried such promise. I remember that, for a moment, as my whole attention focused on that glistening light, I thought it was the knife that Abraham, blessed be his name, held over Isaac. I thought, all in the brief glistening moment, that surely there would appear the ram, from behind the trees, who would save me, that God would spare me and send me home, to my Miriam, as Abraham returned to his Sarah. It flashed through my mind that I, too, was being tested, perhaps for the lust I showed toward my Miriam when awakened in the night, still half asleep. How foolish that I should have thought of Abraham in that moment. But, then, I so trusted that God was watching over me, the way Abraham must have trusted that God would restore his Isaac.

In the next moment, a couple of those boys were holding me tight, from behind. My bag that held my prayer book and my tallis fell to the ground — may God forgive me. I could not help it. My prayer book, which had never touched any floor, let alone the dirt of the earth. As I looked at the blue velvet bag there, down on the ground, all I could think was "I am a sinner, I am a sinner, they are making out of me a sinner."

As they held my hands behind my back, the one with the knife came up in front of me. He was a tall boy, about sixteen, with cold blue eyes, a cold blue like the sky above, dressed poorly in worn clothes, not warm enough for the winter. I felt ashamed, for my worn but warm winter coat with the fur collar and hat and felt that I would have been safer if I were in as threadbare a jacket as he. His blue eyes looked into my face, with hatred. He spit into my face. I remember how the hot wetness of his spit on my face touched my skin, which was frozen with fear, and how, when he lifted the cold knife and placed it against my throat, I felt nothing. Something flowed through me that made my skin numb.

I began to say the Shema — "Hear, O Israel, the Lord our God is One" — for I was certain that these would be the last breaths of my life. But he did not kill me. He took the knife, which must have been very sharp, and lifted it to my chin and cut around my chin, to my neck and close to my ears. He could have cut my ear off. But he did not. He cut only my beard, from my face. They held me from behind, and I helped them and held myself very still, as still as the frozen roots under the ground, as he kept spitting in my face and cutting my beard, his snarling lips muttering "dirty Jew."

The others in the circle watched and laughed. It was a laugh that was mixed with power, as when people are drunk and yet nervous, as if they were not yet quite used to doing this to Jews. Maybe I was their first. At least I was the first in my shtetl. They knew who to come after. If you come for the rebbe, the leader of the flock, all of the others will feel the knife on their throats, as if it were happening to them.

The one who cut my beard off held it up, in one hand, like an animal trophy he had caught in the hunt, and the victory weapon, the knife, he held up, in the other hand, drunk on the power of his act. The two behind me released my hands. With disgust, he delivered the long, brownish red length of my beard into my trembling hands, as if he was handing me my disgrace. He looked into my eyes, with a hatred that had triumphed, and said, "Next time I will kill you, Jew." I do not know why he did not kill me then. Maybe he knew that it would have a longer-lasting effect on my people if I would live for them to see me filled, forever, with this moment of terror.

I held my beard and thought of how I had once held the light body of our stillborn daughter, our only daughter, Leah, who was buried a short distance away, through the trees, at the edge of the meadow. I thought of how her grave must still be covered with snow. At the same time, my whole mind leaped to my prayer book. All I could see was the velvet bag, on the ground. For the first time, the blue velvet looked ominous to me, like the dark, pitch-blue sky before a storm breaks. I could hear my prayer bag calling to me: "Pick me up, pick me up." But I could not move. All I could do was stand there, still frozen, thinking of my dead daughter. In some other corner of my brain, I remember thinking "Poor boys, poor souls," about the younger ones. And then I heard myself say, "My prayer book, my prayer book," reaching with the words even as my body was frozen and could not move.

They left me standing there as they walked away, in the direction of their village. They were finished with me. Now I know that what they were looking for, those poor Polish fellows, was to find someone to make lower than themselves. I see, now, how these boys were the sparks that later burst into the burning hell that was the beginning of the end.

I kept standing there. I could feel that my pants were wet. I could not move. I was crying "My prayer bag, my prayer bag." I do not know if I whispered those words or screamed them. I do not know why I could not move my feet, to reach to the ground. The youngest of them, a thin, scared looking boy, looked back at me. He must have heard me. Quickly, as if he did not want the others to see, he bent to the ground and picked up my bag. Thank the Blessed One. As he came near me, he looked afraid. He brought my prayer bag to me. I somehow reached out my hand and took it. He did not look at my eyes. I remember praying for him, as I saw him walk away, that he should be saved, by his courage, from the violence that he was being swept into.

I stood there, watching, until they became specks in the distance and finally disappeared. It was silent except for the keening sound of the trees as they bent back and forth, like praying men. I remember that which loomed like a dense cloud, the ominous quiet after the storm. I remember the smell of fear, as if a skunk were lurking in the woods. It was the scent of my own fear, and it was all around, inside and outside of me. Only slowly did my senses return, as I stood there, holding my prayer bag, in the palm of my left hand. My beard I held tenderly, in my right hand, like something dying, and rested it on my prayer bag, to give it comfort. Slowly, my breath returned, and I began to breathe freely. I knew what I needed to do.

I walked past the wooded trees, covered with the shadows of late afternoon. I just kept following my feet, walking where they led me. My mind was worried that my Miriam would not know where I was. Never had I been late for the Sabbath before. It had always been such a pleasure to put the dinner on the table, with her, as the light faded. But today was different. I found myself walking in the meadow. I looked up to the open sky. Soon the first star of Shabbos would appear. I went toward the cemetery where my parents and grandparents are buried and my little sweet daughter, Leah.

I bent down, on the cold earth. I prayed David's prayer to God: "I am exceedingly distressed. Let us fall into Hashem's hand, for His mercies are abundant. Favor me, Hashem, for I am feeble. Heal me, Hashem, for my bones shudder. . . . Hashem has heard my plea. Hashem will accept my prayer. . . . Let all my foes be shamed and utterly confounded. They will regret and be instantly shamed."

While I prayed, I dug a hole, with my hands, in the hard earth. I dug so hard, my fingers began to bleed. The hole I dug, next to my daughter's grave. Somehow, I knew, even then, that I would not be there to see the spring flowers come upon her grave. Into the hole, I placed my beard. As I lay it down on the earth, I was sure that I could feel life moving in it. Don't ask me how. I spread it on the earth. As I looked at it, I saw that it was me. But it was not mine. I was me, but it was not me. It was a part of all that had come before me. My father's beard and his father's before him. All the way back to Abraham's beard. This is what I thought even though I did not know what I was thinking. I did not know what I was burying. I only knew that to lose my beard, on that day, was to have the threads severed that wove me to all those who came before. Some mysterious source of power had become lost to me. Suddenly I was cut off and wandering into the desert. Alone. Exiled. This is what was happening to me. In my cells I knew everything, even then, without quite knowing. This is what those boys had done to me instead of killing me.

I covered the earth slowly, as if I were carefully burying a treasure that would one day be found, a rent cloth that would be made whole. I rose and went to place a stone upon each grave, asking that the name of each of my loved ones be a blessing that would follow me. I lingered for a moment and thought of Joseph's bones and how they had been remembered and somehow found and carried through the desert.

I should have walked home quickly, as there were already three or four stars in the heavens. But I walked slowly, delaying getting there, for my Miriam and my sons to see my bare face, to see my soul turned gray, to see my wet pants. I did not want to see the fear and pain upon their faces. I did not want to walk in that door when it was the time for the Shekinah, the Sabbath bride, to enter the doorway and to give us each a second soul, for the Sabbath. I did not want to soil her.

As I walked home, I thought of Miriam and me when we were young, before we were married. How beautiful she was. How we danced in the meadow on those Sabbaths in the springtime, her chestnut hair swaying around her shoulders. Her smiling eyes my face of love.

I knew that Miriam would become filled with fear when she saw me enter the house. She had already been asking me to leave with Label, to sail to America. So many of our landsmen had left already, to make their way and to bring their women and children over. We had heard rumors of terrible things happening in other shtetls. Now, for sure, she would insist. I knew, as I walked home, that I would not see the spring come back to our shtetl. I would not hear the birds. What would happen to us? What would happen? This question gnawed at me as I approached home.

When I reached home, the sky was already dark. I stood outside of the house, for a long time. I stood at the window and looked into the house, through the lace curtains. I could see Miriam and Label and little Chaim, my beautiful wife and sons, sitting at the table. They were so still, seeming not to move, as if they were becoming a painting for me. The whole room was filled with the golden light of the Sabbath candles and with the glow of the two challahs that sat upon the table. I thought I could be looking at the Lord's table. They did not touch the food upon their plates. They sat silently, looking into the candlelight, waiting, worrying. I did not want to stop looking at them from where I stood, for they were entering my heart, like flowers being pressed there.

When I opened the door, I could see the horror on their faces as they looked up at me. They came to me, and held me, their arms around me and mine around them. Together we raised one another up, from the shadows of fear. Miriam placed her two hands upon my face, holding my naked, shamed skin, with her tenderness. I stroked her head, to comfort her. We ate our dinner, in silence. I did not know if the Shekinah dared to be with us. When the Sabbath candles burned down, we sat and planned that Label and I should leave as soon as possible.

Miriam left the table and brought two small, delicate, brass candlesticks to Label. They had been her mother's. She wrapped them in a cloth of lace she had made and, embracing him, told him to carry them and to save them, to give to his wife, for their Sabbath candles. And then Miriam prayed over the candles on our table: "Please God, next year, in America, may it be your will that we sit at my son Label's table, with his bride, with our Chaim, and with my beloved husband, Mordecai."

That night, Miriam and I held one another through the night. Our bare bodies cleaved to one another as they had not in many years. We held one another, reaching to one another, our bodies breathing like one breath, breathing ourselves into one another, that we should remember ourselves as one body, one soul, until we would be together again. Into the space between us, I could sense the Shekinah enter.

Since we married, we had never spent a night apart. Miriam whispered something like a song, over and over again, to me, to herself, to God: "Soon, soon, soon, we will be together. Soon, soon, soon, we will be safe . . . soon . . ."

Over and over again she sang this prayer, like a lullaby, rocking us. I entered her as I had entered my home, that night, entered into a hallowed space, made warm and safe, by our years of smiles and tears. Only, now, knowing that I was being torn from it, there was a desperation to arrive there, and I did so with a fury, as I cried out, "No!"

In the new world, I found a small synagogue to be in with my landsmen. We spent our days wrapped in our talitot, in prayer and study. We sat holding our glasses of hot tea to warm our hearts filled with fear that our loved ones may never join us.

I settled with Label in Brooklyn, New York, in 1904. Label worked hard to earn the money to bring our family to us. I, with my landsmen, spent most of my days in the small synagogue around the corner from where we lived. Together we passed the hours. I sang until the other men sang with me, sang and prayed, sang all the tears in my heart into prayer. I sang all the way to Miriam and all the way to a God I no longer knew had ears to hear. I sang and sang with a longing to melt the place in the center of my heart that had become frozen since that day in the woods. No one knew that that was why I sang, to save myself from the bitter dried desert of my heart. Everyone still called me the zaddika voice, the righteous voice. I did not tell them about the frozen place. They needed me more here than they did back there in our shtetl. And I needed them. Together we kept a spark of the past alive. We made a place, however paltry, to bring our selves and our prayer shawls. When I sang in prayer, I was standing on the earth and under the blue sky of home.

The Voice of Judith

My great-grandmother and her sons did come to America. The brass candlesticks sit on my table on a piece of lace, both passed to me by my grandmother. What happened to Judah's prayer bag and book and shawl, I shall never know. They are covered by the sands of oblivion like so much else and like the so many who did not flee before the storm consumed that shtetl in Boibrke.

During the Passover of my seventieth year, I went to visit Boibrke with family and friends. I carried with me a small vial in which to place some of the earth of my ancestors to be placed in my grave when I am buried. I also wrote a letter of love to place in the earth where they are buried. It was a drizzly day, the earth still hard from the cold of winter and wet from the rain.

There was no trace of anything Jewish to be found in Boibrke. Where was the synagogue that Judah had prayed in? Where was the Jewish cemetery? I asked and someone pointed to a hill covered with trees and grass but with no gravestones. A friend held an umbrella over my head as I dug with my hands into the earth, lifted some soil into the small container I had brought and buried the letter to my ancestors. A delicate bridge of reverence built over time and exile and loss. I left the hillside carrying the earth of my ancestors under my nails. I did not want to wash my hands, did not want to wash away their cell life mixed with the earth and now a part of me.

With the help of our guide, we found the eldest surviving person in Boibrke. She sat propped on her bed, her head and shoulders covered with a shawl, her face wizened. Her daughter sat with her to translate. I sat on a chair at the foot of her bed. "No," she said, "I do not recall the family of the Shtickers." She bent her head low for a while, looking down at her tremulous shriveled hands. We sat in the silence, until she spoke again. She looked deep into my eyes as she said, "I remember the morning the guards took the young Jewish mothers and their children up to the hill where the cemetery used to be and shot them in a mass grave. I took some of them in to my home and hid them." She dropped her head again and closed her eyes.

I sat silent, her words penetrating my marrow. My marrow told me that she was lying. I looked at this woman who was on the threshold of death. I knew in my gut that she was not telling the truth. I sat and wrestled with my feelings. Perhaps where her soul was pure, she was telling the truth. Perhaps with her eyes closed now, this old woman is praying that she be forgiven not to have had the courage to protect some of those desperate mothers and children. In the silence, I looked down at my own hands, at my nails with the dark rich soul soil under them holding those who did not leave Boibrke and who grow still as flowers and grass on that hill where the headstones had been desecrated.

As I sat there, I recalled what Simon Wiesenthal wrote in *The Sunflower* about how a dying German soldier asked his forgiveness and how Wiesenthal responded that it was not for him to forgive. Only the ones who are gone have the right to forgive, and so there could be no forgiveness. I remembered as I looked at this ancient woman in front of me. I searched my soul and could only find these words to say to her: "Thank you for helping my people." Her daughter translated my words and the old woman wept. This was all I could find in my heart to say, praying that in her heart of hearts she longed before her death for there to be a *tikkun* of the horror of her inaction.

When I light the Sabbath candles in the brass holders that sit on my table on the lace cloth, I hold my hands up to the light and I send blessings to my ancestors, to my generations, to those from Canaan and to those from Boibrke and to those embedded under my finger nails that they may receive a drop of holy light on the Sabbath night.

Midrashic Musings on Angels and Blessings

I want to say thank you, from the bottom of my heart, to all those who are here to celebrate this day with me, as I stand at the threshold of my seventieth year: my blood family; my family of friends; my teachers and students; my rabbi, Mark Sameth, who has steadfastly held a space in which I could move from gingerly pointing my finger to the Hebrew letters to pointing my finger to the Torah scroll; Annie Mass and Susan Harris for holding my hand and saying "good, good," as I dared to try trope; and all those from the Pleasantville Community Synagogue and in my life who have so open-heartedly supported me to arrive at this day. You are each a blessing to me.

And I want to thank those who are so palpably here with me, in spirit. I want to thank my ancestors from the shtetl in Boibrke, in the Carpathian mountains. I can almost hear your prayers, your laughter and your tears, rising toward the heavens, through the mountain trees. I want to tell you all: be at rest, all is well, all is good. I want to thank you for the blessing of the blue thread of faith that you have received from your Torah and passed on to my DNA.

Mother, I thank you, for the survival of your irreverent spirit, which never extinguished, no matter how dark it became. I remain a Kaddish to your lusty laughter. Thank you, for all that you gave me to wrestle with, to journey with and to create a blessing with.

Father, when you died it was Shavuot. There was no time to get your tallis, so that you could be buried in it. That made me sad, for I knew how important that was to you. Later, when I asked mother for it, she had already given it to the synagogue. I looked for it there, but it was in a chest, lost and indistinguishable among all the other talitot. Then, you came to me, in a dream, and told me "Judala, now you must make your own tallis." Is that a blessing you gave to me, to go on and make my life by wrestling with my demons and my angels? For that is what the making of a tallis means to me — the making of a person.

Leslie, my daughter, I thank you for being here, if only for a short time, for guiding my vision. The challenge of wrestling with the bitter taste of losing you has made the commandments to taste the sweetness of living only more imperative.

The process of making my tallis is what brought me to this day, to learn and speak in the soul language of my ancestors, to carry forth the blue thread of hoping and dreaming and creating green lands.

For a year, I have been living with Toldot, today's portion of the Torah, reading and studying, writing poetry and prose, turning and being turned by this mythic story. What sense to make of this family saga of blessings stolen and cried out for? What to make of this father Isaac? Is he blind? What is blindness? My father's Hebrew name was also Yitzhak.

What to make of this mother Rebecca? Is she a manipulator, a puppeteer or a seer of truth? My mother's name was Blanche. My father called her Becky. Her Hebrew name was Rifka, Rebecca.

Mothers and fathers wrapped within mothers and fathers. Turning and being turned. Finding meanings for my story through their stories. Entering the world of midrash, waking dreams, hearing voices within voices within voices. When I think I have the meaning, something new comes and turns me toward a facet of their story and my story I have not seen before.

Let me share, with you, some of my thinking, some of my musings.

Isaac, the son on Mount Moriah, almost sacrificed on that mountain by his own father, Abraham. Aviva Zornberg says that Isaac's ashes remained up there, on the mountain, piled on the altar, even though he walked the earth as large as life. Isaac, who, on Mount Moriah, saw the horror of what this life can be. Isaac, who stood in a silence on the edge of annihilation. Isaac, who knew a chaos, a *tohu*, so deep as to be beyond repair. Isaac, whose name means laughter. But to laugh, one must look, and Isaac turned away from seeing.

During this year, I have faced the Isaac within me. The one who does not want to see what I feel cannot be borne. Do you know the Isaac within you?

Jacob, the one who was already wrestling within the womb with his twin, Esau, Jacob, who, years later, in the desert, will dare to dream and wrestle with the angel for the blessing of his true name. Jacob, who will be given the name Israel. Listen, O Israel, all is One. Jacob, the child who carries the thrust toward repair, the one who is destined to journey from *tohu* to *tikkun*, from the shatterings of blinding loss and trauma, toward wholeness and renewal.

During this year, I have faced the Jacob within me and have called him my *neshumah*, my highest and deepest self. Can you sense the Jacob within you, the one who is propelled toward the blessing of wholeness and, in that process, glimpses the Oneness of all things even while you wrestle with all the internal and interpersonal conflicts of being human?

And then there is Esau, the one who lives for survival, who does not know that a life of *shefa*, of abundance, exists and so settles for a bowl of lentils, Esau, the one who needs a Jacob who can hold to the vision of what is possible, even steal for it. Esau, the one within us who needs a Jacob who is willing to continue on the long journey, to make a green land with the dew of heaven. During this year, I have faced the Esau within myself, the part of me who could not envision a green land, who would settle for a bowl of lentils. Do you know Esau within yourself?

Both twins exist within each of us. Each wants the blessing of the wholeness of existence, the physical and spiritual blessing of a full and embodied life.

Rebecca, Isaac's wife, mother of the twins. The one willing to create divisiveness between her sons and even destroy for the sake of the blessing of creation. The one who can dare to bring the opposites of the twins into struggle, for the sake of heaven. The Zohar says that divisiveness for the sake of love is constructive. That is how the world is created and how it continues to be renewed. Rebecca knows that Jacob needs to put on Esau's qualities, in order to become whole, just as Esau needs to feel, within his hairy physical soul, the spiritual soul, the *neshumah* of Jacob.

Rebecca is the one who takes Jacob to the threshold of Isaac's room, from where he must cross over, to begin his own journey. Led there by Rebecca, Jacob stands in front of his father, in his opposing selves and potential for wholeness, wanting to be blessed by his father, at whatever cost. He stands there like any son or daughter, wanting the blessing of the father as they stand at the threshold, at the beginning of their journey.

During this year, I have met the Rebecca within me, the feminine, creative force who is unrelentingly devoted to my becoming whole, who will support and mother me and then lead me to the threshold and thrust me into the unknown, onto my journey toward wholeness. Can you sense the Rebecca within you?

Perhaps Jacob is being guided not only by his mother but also by his angel. It is told that before we are born, an angel shows us our life spread before us and then places a finger over our mouths, and in that moment, we forget all that we saw. That is why we have an indentation above our upper lip, and that is why we sometimes place a finger there, trying to remember something we have forgotten that is somehow unforgettable. It is also told that our angel wants nothing more than for us to unfold, in our life, the unique destiny that has been revealed to us and that only we can fulfill in this life.

Isaac is also at a threshold, the threshold of his blindness. He is at the turning point of seeing or not seeing. If Isaac can see his sons and know them by their true names, he will have come back from the ashes of Mount Moriah. He will have dared to open the closed wells, to see from the depth of his heart, into the hearts of his children. He will have transmitted to his sons that torn-ness need not be unremitting destruction but that an angel can rise out of the ashes. He will have given his sons, and us, the legacy that we can move from blindness to inner vision, thereby transforming suffering to blessing.

What is the blessing a parent gives a child? The blessing of being imagined as she is in all of her being, in all of her possible selves, the ruddy and the smooth selves, seen all the way into her pure soul, thereby speaking her true name. This is the blessing that Jacob grasped for and that Esau cried out for — "Father, do you not have a blessing for me?"

I can never forget that when my father was dying, in his delirium, he took my hand, to smell me, he held me close, to see me. And this quiet man, who did not laugh much, said, "Judala, you will never know how much I love you." He could not let himself die without giving me the blessing of letting me know he saw me. His name was Yitzhak. It was a blessing. It was good.

When my mother was dying, she could no longer speak. I sat by her side, held her hand with one hand and her face with the other. For a long time, I reached into the well of my heart and brought up "My sweet mother, my brave mother, all that I knew of her to be in her life. After so much wrestling with her, for so many years, I was surprised to find nothing left there to bring up but love. Her name was Rifka, and it was a blessing. It was good.

What is this thing called a blessing? Gregory Orr, in his memoir *The Blessing*, tells us that in Hebrew, "blessing" is *"b'racha,"* "to kneel." In modern English, it is the bestowal of a spiritual grace, through a gesture. In Anglo-Saxon, it is *"blestein,"* "to spatter with blood." This blessing seems to be an interweaving of wounding and grace.

The angel may seem like a demon. It may grab you by the neck, as if to destroy you, as it creates you and forces you to the threshold and out into the unknown.

Perhaps Jacob's angel was propelling him, then, to take responsibility for his future — as Rabbi Nachman says, to remember his future. And so Jacob wrestles to cross the many thresholds: the threshold of his mother's womb, the threshold toward his father's blessing, and then the threshold into his desert journey. He travels from turning point to turning point, entering a dark country that is wide open to terror, death, and blessing, where a person can receive a new identity and a new name.

At first we believe that the blessings we receive from our family are our destiny. Jacob believed his destiny was to inherit the earth and its seed and the blessing of Abraham. Yet, he would have to travel far and for a long time to meet himself, in his uncle Laban. He would have to wrestle with his angels and demons before he could receive his true name, Israel. Even then he was still called Jacob for the rest of his life. We receive a glimpse of our whole self, our true name, and still we must journey.

Esau thought his destiny was to receive the blessing of the firstborn, and that was not so. He had to journey forth and take responsibility for shaping his blessing.

I thought my destiny was to be a mother. My journey toward making my blessing began when I lost my child.

What did you think your destiny was to be? What was the blessing of your family? What blessing are you wrestling for, with your demons and your angels?

Abraham was called *"ha-ivri,"* "he who crosses over." To Abraham, God said, *"Lekh-lekh"* — "Go." We are each called *ha-ivri*; we are each brought to our thresholds and told to cross over, to go.

Abraham was also instructed "Walk before me" — *"hitalekh lefanai."* In *The Exile of the Word*, André Neher tells us that the person who journeys turns around, looks behind and imagines that God has been lost. But the truth is that God has gone ahead, by the side roads. He is already waiting on the horizon. Aviva Zornberg describes the horizon as a thing most clearly seen and, at the same time, the thing never to be attained.

Neher also says that perhaps God asks us to go before Him because He is despairing of the world He has created. He says, "Go before Me, don't let Me down, keep going, raise the scattered sparks." Neher raises the question of which silence will we choose, the silence of despair or the silence of creation.

To journey through the wilderness is more than just to survive. It is for the heart never to forget, to cleave passionately and fiercely to the blessing, even though it may only be recalled dimly, like the sight of the blue dye of Gan Eden or how Isaac recalled the scent of the hem of the angel's dress that he held onto even as the angel ran up the ladder and disappeared beyond reach into the heavens. Or like Judah remembered his beard buried in the earth as a burning coal calling, like the bones of Joseph, to be found.

The blessing dimly remembered as the Beloved calls to us to seek its scent, to hear it as it calls out from the silence or laughter or tears of another, or as the summer sun shimmers on a stone under the lake water, or at our simple table as we break bread and drink wine and talk into the evening with others who also long and wrestle for their blessings on this earth.

The poet Samuel Menashe speaks of the journeyer, in this way:

> At the edge
> Of a world
> Beyond my eyes
> Beautiful
> I know Exile
> Is Always
> Green with hope —
> The river
> We cannot cross
> Flows forever

What is this blessing we are given from today's portion? Neher reminds us that the Torah does not begin with aleph, the first letter; it begins with bet, the second letter — *beresheit*. Our beginnings have no beginning. The Torah ends with a lamed, not a tet, not an omega. We have this blessing: our soul always journeying, always beginning, always at a threshold, challenged by our angel, choosing to travel with the dew of heaven and the green of hope.

We read Toldot in the darkest time of the year. In the same dark month comes Chanukah, the Festival of Lights. We are ever journeying toward new being that we cannot yet see beyond the horizon, guided by a hidden seed of light. That is our blessing.

As we journey from our genesis, through our exodus, there is a kind of sacrifice to be made that is different from the one on Mount Moriah. Robert Johnson, in *Balancing Heaven and Earth*, speaks of the sacrifice of giving up one part of our self, for the sake of a greater wholeness thrusting to be born, a sacrifice that is willingly made with grace even though it may be painful.

Today, I am at a threshold. In my seventieth year I am beginning to learn how to sing. When I came to learning trope, I knew that I could not carry a tune. Isaac blinded himself. I deafened myself. I am ready to sacrifice that deafening. Now I am learning to sing. Like a child I am learning to make the simplest sounds. The Hebrew word *"shira"* means both "song" and "prayer." They are sounds from deep in the well of my heart. They are a blessing, and they are good.

And at what threshold are you today? What blessing do you journey toward?

What sacrifice are you called to make, so that your wholeness may live at the center of you and be your true name?

And so this is the tallis I have woven for my seventieth year in honor of my generations. It is told that once upon a time, every tallis had woven into it a blue thread made of a dye that has long since disappeared. It was said that the blue dye came from a snail that lived in the Garden of Eden. Today, we have only the dim memory of that blue thread. It is invisible to us and yet ever a part of us.

The poet William Stafford tells us how important it is never to forget the thread.

The Way It Is

There's a thread you follow. It goes among
things that change. But it doesn't change.
People wonder about what you are pursuing.
You have to explain about the thread.
But it is hard for others to see.
While you hold it you can't get lost.
Tragedies happen; people get hurt
or die; and you suffer and get old.
Nothing you do can stop time's unfolding.
You don't ever let go of the thread.

Biographical Note

Judith Sarah Schmidt, PhD, is a clinical psychologist in private practice in Westchester County, New York. She is co-director of the Center for Intentional Living and teaches in the States and in Europe. She studied Waking Dream Therapy, with Mme. Colette Aboulker-Muscat, in Jerusalem, and also works with trauma. Judith is a poet and prose writer. She has published *How to Cope with Grief* (Bantam Books). Her poems and articles are published in a variety of journals.

Other Poetry and Short Fictions
Available from Time Being Books

866-840-4334
http://www.timebeing.com

Louis Daniel Brodsky *(continued)*
Seizing the Sun and Moon: Volume Three of *The Seasons of Youth*
Shadow War: A Poetic Chronicle of September 11 and Beyond, Volumes One–Five
Showdown with a Cactus: Poems Chronicling the Prickly Struggle
  Between the Forces of Dubya-ness and Enlightenment, 2003–2006
Still Wandering in the Wilderness: Poems of the Jewish Diaspora
The Swastika Clock: Holocaust Poems
This Here's a Merica *(short fictions)*
The Thorough Earth
Three Early Books of Poems by Louis Daniel Brodsky, 1967–1969: *The Easy
  Philosopher, "A Hard Coming of It" and Other Poems*, and *The Foul Rag-
  and-Bone Shop*
Toward the Torah, Soaring: Poems of the Renascence of Faith
A Transcendental Almanac: Poems of Nature
Unser Kampf: Poems of the Final Solution
Voice Within the Void: Poems of *Homo supinus*
With One Foot in the Butterfly Farm *(short fictions)*
The World Waiting to Be: Poems About the Creative Process
Yellow Bricks *(short fictions)*
You Can't Go Back, Exactly

Harry James Cargas *(editor)*
Telling the Tale: A Tribute to Elie Wiesel on the Occasion of His 65th
  Birthday — Essays, Reflections, and Poems

Judith Chalmer
Out of History's Junk Jar: Poems of a Mixed Inheritance

Gerald Early
How the War in the Streets Is Won: Poems on the Quest of Love and Faith

Gary Fincke
Blood Ties: Working-Class Poems
Reviving the Dead

Charles Adès Fishman
Blood to Remember: American Poets on the Holocaust *(editor)*
Chopin's Piano
In the Path of Lightning

CB Follett
Hold and Release

CB Follett *(continued)*
One Bird Falling

Albert Goldbarth
A Lineage of Ragpickers, Songpluckers, Elegiasts & Jewelers: Selected
  Poems of Jewish Family Life, 1973–1995

Robert Hamblin
Crossroads: Poems of a Mississippi Childhood
From the Ground Up: Poems of One Southerner's Passage to Adulthood
Keeping Score: Sports Poems for Every Season

David Herrle
Abyssinia, Jill Rush

William Heyen
Erika: Poems of the Holocaust
Falling from Heaven: Holocaust Poems of a Jew and a Gentile *(Brodsky and Heyen)*
The Host: Selected Poems, 1965–1990
Pterodactyl Rose: Poems of Ecology
Ribbons: The Gulf War — A Poem

Ted Hirschfield
German Requiem: Poems of the War and the Atonement of a Third Reich Child

Virginia V. James Hlavsa
Waking October Leaves: Reanimations by a Small-Town Girl

Rodger Kamenetz
The Missing Jew: New and Selected Poems
Stuck: Poems Midlife

Norbert Krapf
Blue-Eyed Grass: Poems of Germany
Looking for God's Country
Somewhere in Southern Indiana: Poems of Midwestern Origins

Adrian C. Louis
Blood Thirsty Savages

866-840-4334
http://www.timebeing.com

Leo Luke Marcello
Nothing Grows in One Place Forever: Poems of a Sicilian American

Gardner McFall
The Pilot's Daughter
Russian Tortoise

Joseph Meredith
Hunter's Moon: Poems from Boyhood to Manhood
Inclinations of the Heart

Ben Milder
From Adolescence to Senescence: A Life in Light Verse
The Good Book Also Says . . . : Numerous Humorous Poems Inspired by
    the New Testament
The Good Book Says . . . : Light Verse to Illuminate the Old Testament
Love Is Funny, Love Is Sad
What's So Funny About the Golden Years
The Zoo You Never Gnu: A Mad Menagerie of Bizarre Beasts and Birds

Charles Muñoz
Fragments of a Myth: Modern Poems on Ancient Themes

Brenda Marie Osbey
History and Other Poems

Micheal O'Siadhail
The Gossamer Wall: Poems in Witness to the Holocaust

Charles Rammelkamp
Fūsen Bakudan: Poems of Altruism and Tragedy in Wartime

Joseph Stanton
A Field Guide to the Wildlife of Suburban Oʻahu
Imaginary Museum: Poems on Art

Susan Terris
Contrariwise